HUNGARIANS IN THE AMERICAN CIVIL WAR BY EUGENE PIVÁNY

ILLUSTRATED BY

JOHN KEMÉNY.

REPRINTED FROM DONGÓ TENTH ANNIVERSARY NUMBER

CLEVELAND. OHIO

1913

Reprinted 2012

ISBN 978-1-105-63773-5

Publisher's Note

This long, historical article appeared in the Cleveland-based Hungarian magazine Dongó in 1913. As no translator is credited, it may have appeared originally in English.

It appears the article was reissued as a stand-alone pamphlet, which is what you now hold in your hands.

This is not a facsimile edition and in resetting the type we have tried to capture all accent marks.

The images here are at least a generation removed from the originals, however. The captions are as they appeared in the original.

Unlike the original reprint, which showed footnotes, we have changed these to end notes, the only major alteration to the original organization of the material

The unique subject matter is well-worth preserving in a reprint edition and we hope that you find this book enjoyable and useful.

Frontpiece from the 1913 Pamphlet

Table of Contents

Hungarians in the American Civil War

Part I

Although the Hungarian has but recently become an "element" in the great American "melting pot," he has been by no means a stranger on this continent. He seems to have even preceded here all European races except the Norsemen, for the *Tyrker*, or Turk, who, according to the Icelandic saga, discovered grapes at Vinland about the year 1000 A.D., could have been no other than an Hungarian[i]. In Sir Humphrey Gilbert's ill-fated expedition to New Foundland in 1583 we find an Hungarian humanist, Stephanus Parmenius Budaeus, who had been selected by Sir Humphrey, on account of his learning and his elegant Latin verse, to be the historian of the expedition. Even the "fake" Hungarian nobleman appeared quite at the beginnings of colonial history, the first known example of this, fortunately not very numerous, species being no less a personage than the redoubtable Captain John Smith, President of Virginia, Admiral of New England, etc. He alleged to have received a patent of nobility, or grant of arms, from Sigismund Báthory, Prince of Transylvania, a copy of which is on file in the College of Arms in London. Hungarian historians, however, pronounced it to be a forgery, and a very clumsy one at that.

There are records of Hungarian settlers and travelers all through the colonial period and the first half -century of the United States. But they are only sporadic instances, as the Hungarians were not a sea-faring people and have never made any systematic attempt at colonization; in fact, all the energy they possessed was needed in their own country to hold their own against the encroachments of the Habsburgs on their liberties. Of the Hungarian travelers who visited the United States in the first half of the nineteenth century, the most prominent was Alexander Farkas de Bölön, whose book, first published at

Kolozsvár in 1834, and particularly his observations on the political institutions of the American republic, made a deep impression on the Hungarian mind, the more so as they had a direct bearing on the political reforms then advocated in Hungary. Farkas's book was, no doubt, also one of the causes that induced an ever increasing number of Hungarians to emigrate to the American Land of Promise in the thirties and forties of the nineteenth century; they were, however, still too few to engage the attention of the statistician.

Hungary was then in the ferment of a grand liberal movement, in which the three greatest Hungarians of the century, Széchényi, Kossuth and Deák, took a leading part. This movement culminated in the upheaval of 1848, which, starting in France, swept over the whole continent of Europe. It was successful only in France. The liberals of the German and Italian countries, with the exception of Venice, soon had to drop their swords. Hungary alone kept up the struggle for a year and a half, and was finally overcome only by the combined efforts of the two greatest military powers of the age. It was not merely the traditional military prowess and patriotic self-sacrifice of the Hungarians, admirable as they were, that made their magnificent struggle possible; in these qualities the other peoples may not have been much behind them. It was their inbred constitutional instinct; it was their possession of a constitution which, alone on the Continent, was not a single written instrument based on the experiences of others, or the gift of a benevolent ruler, but was — like the English constitution — ^the natural growth of many centuries, making the sovereign nation the source of all legitimate authority; it was their experience in self-government in the counties which — when the rest of Europe was groaning under the weight of feudalism — were semi-independent little republics; in short, it was their possession of free institutions and the memories of the blood and treasure which their fathers had spent in securing and defending them, that enabled the Hungarians to rally around their leader and to keep the banner of liberty flying long after the others had failed.

The glorious Hungarian Honvéd Army was the hope and the object of admiration of the whole civilized world, and nowhere more so than in the United States. President Taylor acted only in accord with public sentiment when he dispatched Ambrose Dudley Mann, of Virginia, as special and confidential agent to Hungary to ascertain the true state of affairs with the view of recognizing her independence. Mann's reports, published only recently[ii] are eloquent testimonials of American sympathy for the Hungarian cause, and offer a refreshing contrast to the reports of Lord Ponsonby, the British ambassador to Vienna, who appears to have been the dupe of Prince Schwarzenberg.

Hungary, at last, had to yield to the overwhelming power of Russia. Some of the patriots went into exile at once; others fell the victims of Austria's insane vengeance; still others, seeing the fate of their brothers who had stayed at home, kept in hiding, waiting for an opportunity to flee to foreign countries. Most of those who followed Kossuth to Kutahia and Bem to Aleppo eventually came to the United States to join, or to be joined later by, their fellow-exiles who had found refuge first in Turkey, Italy, France or England. Louis Kossuth himself was freed from his confinement in Kutahia by the United States and taken on board a national vessel. There was a veritable Hungarian cult in America in 1849 and the early fifties, which, when Kossuth reached New York harbor in December, 1851, "had become almost a frenzy."

Since the Hungarians who, a decade later, offered their lives for the preservation of the American Union, came mainly from among these refugees, some observations on the character of this Hungarian immigration will not be out of place. It stands in a class by itself among all the immigrations of the nineteenth century. Its causes were purely political; its members came mostly from the middle and upper classes, and were thus superior in education and character to the average immigrant; they had received knowledge of self-government as an inheritance from their ancestors; they had seen actual service on the field of war; they were firm believers in democratic institutions, and they considered the United States as truly the Land of the Free.

Of course, there were many immigrants of other races in the same class, and the relations of the Hungarian, German, Bohemian and Polish refugees were very cordial, if not fraternal. But the other refugees were only a small minority of their countrymen who, particularly the Germans and the Irish, immigrated in the fifties in unprecedented numbers, being assisted therein by societies organized especially for that purpose. Some German dreamers even conceived fanciful plans for making German states out of Missouri and Wisconsin.

The Hungarian immigration was entirely unorganized. The refugees generally arrived in small groups and, more often than not, met with a sympathetic reception, helpful advice or even financial assistance from noble-hearted Americans. Not infrequently they were ceremoniously welcomed, entertained by the authorities, and lionized by Society. At first they hoped to be called back soon to take up anew the fight for the independence of their country, but before long they realized that events in Europe were drifting in an unfavorable direction for such action. Within a few years they were scattered all through the free states as farmers, engineers, journalists, lawyers, merchants, teachers, clerks, etc., ultimately attaining more or less success and becoming respected citizens of their several communities.

Very few of them settled in the slave-holding states, except Missouri, as they instinctively detested slavery and were unwilling to employ slave labor. Probably the most prominent of the refugees was Ladislaus Ujházy, the scion of a noble race, former Lord Lieutenant of Saros County and Commissioner of the District of Komarom, who in America was generally called "Governor" Ujházy. He first founded an Hungarian settlement named New Buda in Iowa, but, having lost his wife there, moved to Texas where he and his children built their own house and cultivated their own land. He did not take part in the Civil War, having been appointed United States Consul at Ancona by President Lincoln in 1861.

Another distinguished refugee was Col. John Prágray who had been Adjutant-General of the Honvéd Army. He arrived in New York in December, 1849, and, assisted by a fellow-exile, Cornelius Fornet, immediately set himself to the task of writing a history of the Hungarian War[iii]. This was the first English book on the subject, it had a wide circulation and, although necessarily imperfect and partizan, it was used as an authority in the subsequent flood of English literature dealing with the Hungarian question. Noble Prágray! He found an opportunity sooner than most of his fellows to offer his sword for the cause of liberty. He joined Narciso Lopez's ill-fated expedition for the liberation of Cuba, was severely wounded in the engagement at Las Pozas on the second anniversary of the surrender at Világos (August 13, 1851), and, to escape the ignominy of the *garote*, ended his life with his own hand before the Spanish soldiers could take him prisoner*[iv].

Part II

When the conflict between national unity and states' rights and between freedom and slavery came to an issue which could be fought out only on the field of battle, the Hungarians in America responded liberally to the call for volunteers. They came of a race proud of its military qualities; most of them, as we have seen, had taken part in the Hungarian War, some of them also in the Crimean and Austro-Italian Wars; they were devoted to the cause of liberty; they felt grateful for the sympathy shown their native land in its hour of distress and for the honors showered upon their late chief, Louis Kossuth. No wonder they were eager to enlist in the Union Army; no wonder they did useful, honorable and glorious service on the battlefield for their adopted country.

Figure 1 Where Kossuth rode up Broadway, December 6, 1851

As already stated, hardly any of them had settled in the slave-holding states; consequently, hardly any of them enlisted in the Confederate Army. In fact, the only Hungarian officer I have found record of on the southern side was B. Estván, Colonel of Cavalry. Having served in the Austrian Army under Radetzky in Italy and taken part in the Crimean War (presumably in the British Army) he could not well resist the call of his southern neighbors and friends to take up arms in behalf of their cause. But at heart he was a Unionist, and he ended his dilemma by resigning his commission as soon as he could do so with honor, and going to England. There he related his experiences in the South in an interesting book which was published in London, New York and Leipzig in 1863[v].

It would be interesting to know the number of Hungarians in the United States at the outbreak of the Civil War and the number of Hungarian soldiers in the Union Army. For the former we should naturally look to the census of 1860, but with disappointing results, for that census — at least as far as the nativity of the population is concerned — was not made up on scientific principles. Hungarians were not treated separately, and even Austria appeared only as a subdivision of "Germany." It is very likely that the Hungarians were included among the 25,061 shown as Austrians, although — as Secretary of State Seward aptly remarked[vi] — there were no *confessed Austrians* in America. Nearly one-third of these Austrians lived in Wisconsin, where German colonization was carried on systematically; so it is fair to presume that the majority were Austrian Germans.

We get more enlightenment from the census of 1870, in which the natives of the Dual Monarchy appear in a trialistic arrangement: Austria (proper) 30,508, Bohemia 40,289, and Hungary 3,737. The Hungarian immigration from 1866 to 1870 was so small as to be negligible (officially reported as 79), because this was a period of revival in Hungary, when many exiles returned to their native land, taking advantage of the political amnesty announced on the re-establishment of the constitution in 1867. This small immigration was undoubtedly more than offset by the deaths and re-migrations of the decade; we can not err much, then, if we estimate the average number of Hungarians during the war at 4,000. This is hardly more than a drop in the bucket, considering that the total free population of the United States in 1860 was 27,489,461, of whom 23,353,286 were natives and 4,136,175 foreign-born. Of the latter about 1,300,000 were Germans.

It is more difficult to answer our second question : What was the number of the Hungarian soldiers in the Union Army? The original muster-rolls are, for very good reasons, now practically inaccessible; and even if they were not, no complete record of the nativity of the men could be obtained from them, for the state or country of birth was not systematically required on the enlistment rolls until the Provost Marshal General's Bureau began its activity, after the war had been waged for some time. Often the place of residence was given instead of the place of birth. Francis B. Heitman's *Historical Register and Dictionary of the U. S. Army* is a very useful compilation, stating the nativity of the general and staff officers ; but it refers only to officers and, as I have had occasion to find out, is far from complete. The rosters published by the various states shed little light on the subject, for as a rule they contain no data as to the nativity of the men.

Shortly after the war, the U. S. Sanitary Commission started an investigation on these lines, which was under the direction of its actuary, Benj. Apthorp Gould. He was assisted by a large staff and had, to a certain extent, the cooperation of the War Department and the Adjutants-General of the various states. For more than half the enlistments he got the official figures, for nearly 300,000 men he obtained data from various commanders, and the rest he estimated in the proportions thus arrived at. His figures, while necessarily not exact, are more trustworthy than any other calculations made on the subject, and are given here for their general interest, although they contain no specific information about Hungarians. They refer only to white soldiers in the Union Army, and leave out of consideration 92,000 men from certain western states and territories.

Natives 1,523,267

Germans 176,817

Irish 144,221

British Americans [Canadians] 53,532

English 45,508

Other Foreigners 48,410

"Foreigners" not otherwise designated 26,445

[Total foreigners]	494,933
Grand total	2,018,200[vii]

These are impressive figures, but it is to be borne in mind that they do not take account of the numerous re-enlistments. As to Hungarians, their number was so small that the statistician, who deals with quantity rather than quality, did not consider them separately. We have to resort, then, to other means to make an estimate of their number.

Nearly one-half of the Garibaldi Guard or 39th New York Infantry[viii] and about one-half of the Lincoln Riflemen, incorporated later in the 24th Illinois Infantry[ix], were Hungarians. This makes about 400. For additional data I examined the published regimental rosters of some of the states, only one of which (Iowa) contained records of the nativity of the men. It was a rather unsatisfactory investigation, because there was nothing to go by but the names. The Hungarians being a composite race, many of them have non-Hungarian names ; many of the refugees, on fleeing their country, changed their names; many of the names were misprinted or had undergone more or less recognizable changes toward "Anglicisation." Nevertheless I found about a hundred Hungarian names in the regiments of Iowa, Ohio and part of Illinois. So I believe that the total number of Hungarian soldiers could not have been much above or much below 800, of whom from 80 to 100 were officers.

This is certainly a small number compared with the imposing figures above quoted. But it is about 20 per cent, of the Hungarian population, a ratio not approached by any of the other races and explainable only by the unique character of the Hungarian immigration of that period. And could anything prove more the eminent military fitness of the Hungarians than that this handful of men produced

2 major-generals,

5 brigadier-generals,

15 colonels,

2 lieutenant-colonels,

13 majors,

12 captains,

... besides a number of subaltern officers and two surgeons. General Stahel commanded an army corps, General Asbóth a division and a district, General Schoepf a division and a fort; while Generals Knefler, Kozlay, Mundee and Pomucz and Colonel Zsulavszky had charge of brigades.

The appended partial list contains the public records, more or less complete, of 61 officers. In compiling this list and the biographical sketches, use was made of Heitman's Register, the Official Army Register of the Volunteer Force of the U.S. Army, Dyer's Compendium of the War of the Rebellion, reports of the Adjutants-General of several states, and the Rebellion Record; also of various English, Hungarian and German books, memoirs, magazine and newspaper articles, and the oral or written communications of some of the participants or their descendants. No claim is made to absolute accuracy or completeness; and any correction or additional information will be gratefully received.

Part III

Since the Hungarians, few as they were, were scattered all over the country, enlisted from nearly every state and served in various armies, departments and corps, it is impossible to present their story in a continuous narrative. We must be satisfied, therefore, with individual sketches, unconnected, or but loosely connected at the best.

There was no purely Hungarian organization in the Union Army. The nearest to one were the Garibaldi Guard of New York and the Lincoln Riflemen of Chicago. The latter were organized as an independent company of Hungarians and Bohemians by Geza Mihalóczy, a former honvéd officer, with another Hungarian, Augustus Kovats, as his lieutenant. This was in February, 1861, more than two months before Lincoln's first call for troops; and the far-seeing Mihalóczy drilled his men night after night to be prepared when the call should come. His request to the President-elect to permit the company to be named after him was presented to Mr. Lincoln at Springfield, 111., by Julian Kuné, also a honvéd officer, and was gladly granted. Within 48 hours from the receipt of Gov. Yates' order to send a force to Cairo, Gen. Swift left Chicago with several companies, among them the Lincoln Riflemen.

In Cairo there was much confusion at first, owing to the lack of experienced officers and the untrained condition of the troops. This was partly overcome by the energy of Gen. McClellan, who wrote[x] that "the artillery, especially, made very good progress under the instruction of Col. Wagner, an Hungarian officer, whom I had sent there for that object." Col. Gustave Wagner had been a major of artillery in the Honvéd Army, and accompanied Governor Kossuth co Kutahia. He was the son of a heroic mother, for it was his mother who, under great personal danger, returned from Turkey to Hungary, and, in disguise and with a false passport, effected the escape of Mme. Kossuth from Hungary.

He was in charge of the expeditions to Belmont and Lucas Bend, Mo., and when he was appointed chief of ordnance on Gen. Fremont's staff. Gen. U.S. Grant wrote to Fremont that "his loss from this post will be felt." Later, he commanded the 2nd New York Artillery. William Howard Russell, war-correspondent of the London Times, spoke of him and the other Hungarians in Missouri (in his Pictures of Southern Life) as of "a fine, soldierly-looking set of men." The soldierly looks of the Hungarians were commented on also by several other writers of the period.

In the West it was of vital importance to secure the two border states, Missouri and Kentucky, for the Union and to free the Mississippi from Confederate control. In St. Louis, independently of the volunteer regiments raised for the Federal army, several regiments of Home Guards (a literal translation of the word Honvéd) were organized "for the protection of the home and family, for the free exercise of the franchise and the supremacy of the Union," the leading idea being "to make this body strong enough to prevent even the chance of a fight within the limits of the city." The plan originated with three Hungarians, Anselm Albert, Robert and Roderick Rombauer, who met early in January, 1861, to form such an organization. Eventually five regiments of such Home Guards were organized in St. Louis. They not only fully accomplished their object, but sometimes volunteered to do duty outside of the city also, and were known officially as the U.S. Reserve Corps, Missouri Volunteers. The tactical development of the first regiment was attended to by Lieut.-Col. Robert J. Rombauer, and that of the second regiment by Lieut.-Col. John T. Fiala, who had also been a honvéd officer.

Anselm Albert had served in the Engineering Corps of the Honvéd Army as lieut.-colonel, after Vilagos followed Gen. Bem to Aleppo, and came to the United States in 1850, where he eventually settled in St. Louis. He was lieut.-colonel of the 3d Missouri Infantry, became an aide-de-camp to Gen. Fremont in the West with the rank of colonel and later his chief-of-staff in the Mountain Department.

The Rombauers are a remarkable family. Originally of Saxon stock, they settled in Hungary some 500 years ago, and gave several prominent citizens and stanch patriots to Hungary. Theodore Rombauer was director of the Hungarian Government's ammunition factory at Nagy Varad during the revolution, and, after the surrender of Gen. Gorgei, had to flee for his life. Four of his sons had served the Hungarian cause, and four of his sons fought in the Union Army. They were, however, not the same four sons, for one of them, Richard, had lost his life in the battle of Vizakna, in Transylvania, and his place was taken in America by a younger brother.

Robert J. Rombauer, the oldest son, was an artillery lieutenant in the Honvéd Army. When that army was crushed by the Russians, he stayed in the country, believing, like many others, that it would be impossible for Austria to wreak vengeance on every subaltern officer. He was mistaken, however, for he was taken prisoner and pressed into the Austrian Army as a private. After ten months his devoted mother succeeded in getting his release, and the whole family was soon re-united in Iowa, whence, after an unsuccessful effort at farming, they moved to St. Louis in 1853. There, as already stated, he took a leading part in organizing the Home Guards, and, when their term expired, re-enlisted for three years, becoming colonel of the 1st U.S. Reserve Corps, Missouri Volunteers. In 1863 he published a military treatise[xi] and in the centennial year of St. Louis a history of the conflict in St. Louis during 1861, with a thoughtful and judicious review of the causes leading to the Civil War, as an introduction[xii]. He was also engaged in journalism and held several offices of trust and honor in St. Louis, as President of the Board of Assessors. member of the School Board, Commander of the Grand Army of Missouri, etc. Now, at the patriarchal age of eighty-two, he is still hale and hearty, and devotes himself to literary work.

Roderick E. Rombauer, although at that time "wretchedly poor" (as he states in his autobiography[xiii]), managed to study law at Harvard, and returned to St. Louis in 1858. He was a struggling lawyer when the Civil War broke out, and enlisted as a private in the 1st Missouri Infantry and was afterwards commissioned captain. His company took part in the capture of Camp Jackson and did some service in Southeast Missouri, when he was taken violently ill with camp fever. After his recovery he served on Gen. Fremont's staff in West Virginia for several months. In 1863, after an exciting personal canvass, he was elected judge of the Law Commissioners Court of St. Louis County, which was the beginning of a very successful judicial career, in the course of which he became judge of the Circuit Court and of the Court of Appeals. In 1897 he returned to his law practice and, although he has nearly reached four-score, is still at his desk every day. Of magnetic personality, he is a forceful and popular public speaker, a publicist of note, and recognized as one of the ablest jurists of Missouri.

Roland T. Rombauer enlisted also in St. Louis, served as sergeant in the 1st Missouri Infantry, commanded a battery in Virginia, became captain of the 1st Florida Cavalry and Provost Marshal of the District of West Florida under Gen. Asboth. After the war, he was active in politics, and was a delegate to the Republican National Convention of 1868 and a member of the Montana Legislature. He was a successful mining engineer and the author of several treatises on mining.

The youngest brother, Raphael Guido Rombauer, was sergeant in the Home Guard, and became Major of the 1st Illinois Light Artillery and an aide on Gen. Grant's staff. He was an engineer, and was at one time superintendent of the Southwest Branch of the Missouri Pacific Railroad. Later he engaged in coal-mining, and was at the head of the Rombauer Coal Company at Kirksville, Mo., when he died in 1912.

Part IV

Towards the end of July, 1861, General John C. Fremonr took command of the Western Department, comprising Missouri, Kansas, Illinois and Kentucky, with headquarters at St. Louis. His pioneer work in the exploration of the Rocky Mountains, which gained him the title of Pathfinder, his part in the conquest of California, his romantic marriage, and his gallant fight as the first presidential candidate of the Republican Party, had made him one of the most popular men of the period. Most of his critics believe that he was not the right man for the organization and command of a whole army. Yet it is certain that in the agitation and intrigues, which lead to his temporary removal after exactly one hundred days of command, both politics and the unreasonable expectation of quick and decisive results with inadequate means, had a prominent part. He was also often criticised for appointing many foreign-born officers. Yet there was no other way open for him, for there were no militia organizations in the West, and he could get but a few West Point graduates. Most of his officers had to be selected from among "green" native civilians and the foreign-born citizens who had had military experience abroad[xiv]. Whatever his shortcomings may have been, even his severest critics admit that he was a man of charming personality, able to win and hold the devotion of his men and to fire them with enthusiasm.

Of his staff officers the following were Hungarians: Brig.-Gen. Alexander Asboth, Chief -of- Staff; Col. John T. Fiala, Chief Topographical Engineer; Col. Gustave Wagner, Chief of Ordnance; Major Charles Zagonyi, Commander of the Body Guard; Col. Anselm Albert, Capt. Leonidas Haskell and Capt. Joseph Reményfi, Aides-de-Camp.

Col. Fiala was one of the ablest engineers in the country. Born at Temesvar, Hungary, in 1822, he received his education at the Military Academy of Gratz, Austria, joined the Honvéd Army in 1848, and attained the rank of major. He followed Gen. Bem to Syria, after whose death he sought refuge in France, but left that country for the United States in 1851. He made and published the first large sectional and topographical map of Missouri, and suggested to Gen. Lyon the St. Louis forts subsequently built by Fremont. Gen. Fremont entertained a high opinion of this officer's abilities, and had him appointed on his staff again when he got command of the Mountain Department the following year. There Col. Fiala was seized with a dangerous disease and had to retire from the service. Although the army surgeons had given up his life, he recovered under the care of a physician in Davenport, Iowa, and settled eventually in San Francisco, where he ended his useful life in 1911.

Figure 2 John T. Fiala

Toward the end of September, Gen. Fremont moved to Jefferson City, whence he began his march southward to Springfield. His Army of the West contained approximately 50,000 men in five divisions, the fourth of which, with about 6,500 men, was under the command of Gen. Asboth. After crossing the Osage River, the Prairie

Scouts, a mounted body of about 150 men under Major Frank White, a gallant officer hardly out of his teens, and a detachment of Fremont's Body Gnurd, about 150 mounted men, under Major Charles Zágonyi, were sent forward to reconnoitre in the direction of Springfield.

Charles Zágonyi was born at Szatmar, Hungary, in 1826, espoused the national cause in 1848, and rose to be captain of hussars in Gen. Bern's army in Transylvania. He was wounded and taken prisoner in an engagement, and spent two years in an Austrian dungeon before his escape to America. He was the true representative of that superb type of light cavalrymen which Hungary has given to the world: The Hussars. Imbued with the spirit of ancient chivalry, full of dash, devoted to his commander and able to impart his spirit to his men, he was eminently fit for the position for which Fremont selected him. He was to organize a company of horse to act as the General's bodyguard, but so many were the applicants that four companies were organized. The men were clad in blue jackets, trousers and caps. They were armed with light German sabres, the best that at that time could be procured, and with revolvers; besides which, the first company carried carbines. They were mounted upon bay horses, carefully chosen from the government stables by Zágonyi, who, in less than a month's time, drilled his men into a well-disciplined and efficient corps of cavalry. Their uniforms were simple enough compared with the braided dolmans and breeches of the Hungarian hussars, but to their poorly equipped comrades they looked "showy." Instilled with pride and esprit de corps by Zágonyi, the Guards carried themselves rather proudly and were dubbed holiday soldiers by the envious This attitude of ridicule towards the Guard, however, was soon to be changed into one of respect and admiration.

The officers were all Americans, except three, — one Dutchman and two Hungarians, Zágonyi and Lieut. Theodore Majthényi.

Zágonyi got permission from Fremont to attack the Confederate garrison at Springfield, which was thought to number about 300. When report was received that it was

1,900 strong, the General revoked his permission, but finally was persuaded by Zágonyi's appeals to let him go, promising to send him reinforcements. Fremont was afraid that the impetuous hussar would do something "rash"; Gen. Sigel also entertained such fears, and sent Zágonyi word not to make an attack until he could send him aid. Sigel's note, however, reached Zágonyi only after it was all over.

Major White, having been taken sick, was left with a few men in a farmhouse, and Zágonyi took command of both troops. On approaching Springfield they saw the enemy's infantry, about 1,200 strong, posted on top of a hill, with about 300 horse on the left and a little lower. To reach the field they had to pass a narrow lane lined with underbrush, cross a brook, and jump a fence. Zágonyi halted his men and told them that, if any of them was tired or sick, he could turn back. No one moved. Then he said: "Our honor, the honor of our General and our country, tell us to go on. I will lead you. We have been called holiday soldiers for the pavements of St. Louis; today we will show that we are soldiers for the battle. Your watchword shall be: The Union and Fremont! Draw sabre! By the right flank, — quick trot, — march!" Little did the honest hussar think that this little speech would be given a sinister meaning by the General's enemies.

The underbrush lining the lane was packed with Confederate sharpshooters. It took the Guards only a minute to dash through the lane, but when they emerged at the other end, some fifty bodies of men and horses were writhing in the lane ; the sharpshooters had done murderous work. On reaching the field, Zágonyi ordered Lieut. Majthényi with thirty men to attack the enemy's cavalry to their right. "With sabres flashing over their heads, the little band of heroes spring towards their tremendous foe. Right upon the centre they charge. The dense mass opens, the blue coats force their way in, and the whole Rebel squadron scatter in disgraceful flight through the cornfields in the rear. The boys follow them, sabring the fugitives."

Zágonyi then charged with the rest of his men the infantry on the hill. "Steeds respond to the ardor of their riders, and quick as thought, with thrilling cheers, the noble hearts rush into the leaden torrent which pours down the incline. With unabated fire the gallant fellows press through. Their fierce onset" is not even checked.

The foe do not wait for them, — they waver, break and fly." The Guardsmen follow them to the village. Zágonyi leads them. A desperate hand-to-hand fight ensues, ending with the utter rout of the enemy.

Part V

It may have been a "rash" act, but it was a glorious victory and one of the most heroic deeds recorded in the annals of warfare[xv]. It was generally referred to as "Zágonyi's death-ride," and Gen. Fremont wrote to his wife: "This was really a Balaklava charge." It is now officially designated as a "skirmish," but it is certain that no skirmish has ever had such moral effect as this one, for it gave tone and spirit to the western army, instilled courage and a feeling of safety into the hearts of the loyal population of Missouri, and had a much-needed, bracing effect all the country over.

Mrs. Fremont jotted down in what she kindly called Zágonyi's "quaint Hungarian-English" his ideas on the subject of "rashness." He said: "They call it a 'rash act.' How is it possible to say it so? From half -past eleven till half -past four we knew we were to meet nineteen hundred men, was time enough to consider and cool down every rashness. Blood cools in five hours. It is so. Very naturally it could not be 'rashness.'"

A week later Gen. Fremont was removed from the command of the Western Department and replaced by Gen. Hunter. The Guard was shamefully treated for its heroism. On its return to St. Louis, it was denied rations and forage, and was promptly disbanded by order of Gen. McClellan. The wild rumors about Fremont's alleged dictatorial ambitions and the "dangerous sentiments" said to be uttered by the Guardsmen were prob ably responsible for these acts. Zágonyi was offered the colonelcy of a regiment, but out of loyalty to his general he declined it. The following year, however, he served again on Gen. Fremont's staff in the East. Mrs. Fremont, in her mortification and to aid the families of the fallen Guardsmen, wrote a story of the Guard, a book charming by its directness and interesting for the many letters not published elsewhere[xvi].

Theodore Majthényi, Zágonyi's gallant lieutenant, was the son of Baron Joseph Majthényi, a prominent refugee, and was but a boy when they made their new home in Davenport, Iowa, in 1851. After the Guard was disbanded, he obtained a commission as captain in the 1st Indiana Cavalry, and in 1866 he entered the regular army as lieutenant in the 6th United States Cavalry. His father returned to Hungary on the re-establishment of the Hungarian constitution, and persuaded him to go with him. There he enlisted in the new Honvéd Army; but he was too much Americanized to like the conditions in Europe, and returned to the United States about 1875.

Gen. Hunter not finding any enemy in the vicinity, decided to return with his army to St. Louis. It was a sad retreat and harmful in its effects, as it undid nearly all that Fremont had accomplished and left the loyal population of Southern Missouri unprotected against the guerrilla bands of the Confederates. Gen. Curtis, who soon replaced Hunter in command, had to do Fremont's campaign over again, and under more unfavorable conditions, because of the cold weather. He had hardly more than 12,000 men in his army, which was composed of four divisions, the second division being under the command of Gen. Asbóth. Two other ex-honvéds had commands under Curtis : Major Emeric Mészáros, who commanded the Fremont Hussars or 4th Missouri Cavalry, and Col. Joseph Németh, in command of the Benton Hussars or 5th Missouri Cavalry. Col. Németh had been a captain in the Honvéd Army, and in Kossuth's suite at Kutahia.

Figure 3 Zágonyi's death ride at Springfield, Mo., Oct. 25, 1861

Gen. Curtis re-occupied Springfield without opposition about the end of February, 1862, and thence, with continued skirmishing, followed the enemy under Generals Price and McCulloch over the border into Arkansas. Gen. Asbóth occupied Fayetteville and Bentonville with little resistance, but was soon ordered to join the main army at Pea Ridge, or Elkhorn Tavern, where a decisive engagement was expected. The first day of the battle, March 7, was very sanguinary, but undecisive. Gen. Asbóth was wounded in the left arm, but in spite of his wound was again in the saddle the next morning[xvii]. The enemy, however, whose numbers were variously estimated as from 16,000 to 26,000, had suffered more, particularly on its right wing and through the death of Gen. McCulloch, and was badly defeated in the second day's fighting. This ended the campaign which secured Missouri for the Union and in which several Hungarian officers had had a distinguished part.

Alexander Asbóth came from a family prominent in the history of Hungary. He was bom in Keszthely on December 18, 1811, and had from childhood on the ambition of becoming a soldier, like his elder brother Louis (who became a general in the Hungarian War.) His mother, however, was averse to the thought of exposing both of her sons to the dangers of a military career, and persuaded him to study engineering. Yet Fate willed that he should fight on the battlefields of two hemispheres and achieve his greatest success as a soldier. After graduating from the Engineering Academy at Selmecbánya, he entered the government service, and had already made himself a national reputation when the revolution of 1848 broke out. He enlisted as a honvéd, became colonel in the Engineering Corps, and, later, aide to Governor Kossuth. He followed the Governor to Kutahia, and was brought to this country on the U. S. Frigate Mississippi in 1851. In New York he met with some success as the inventor of a new process for making steel castings, and was also a surveyor in the service of New York State. John C. Fremont, who had known him in New York, was so favorably impressed with him that, when he was assigned to the command of the Western Department, he selected Asbóth for his chief-of-staff and appointed him brigadier-general.

The Senate considered this appointment — like several others that Fremont had made — "irregular" and refused to confirm it until the report of Asbóth's gallantry at the battle of Pea Ridge was received. In the meantime, however, as we have seen, he was actually in command of a division under Fremont, Hunter and Curtis. He was a tall, well-built man, with a firm, but kindly expression in his face, over which would, at times, come a shadow of melancholy, probably when he was thinking of the fate of his native land. Yet he was essentially a man of action, and enjoyed hard, physical exercise. Major W. Dorsheimer described him as an excellent horseman, who, at the age of fifty, loved to ride his horse at top speed, so that the Major, who was considerably younger, could not keep up with him.

Figure 4 Alexander Asbóth, Brevet Major general, USV

After the Missouri campaign he was assigned to the command of the District of Columbus in Kentucky, and in 1863 was appointed commander of the District of West Florida, with headquarters at Fort Pickens, near Pensacola, which command he held until August, 1865. In the engagement at Marianna (September 27, 1864), he rushed forward to encourage his retreating soldiers. The battle was won, but he was seriously wounded, one bullet shattering his right arm and another lodging under his right cheekbone. He was breveted major-general in March, 1865, for gallant and meritorious service.

Asbóth was one of those generals whom the Government wished to reward for their distinguished services with a diplomatic post. Although there was much dickering about such appointments, his nomination as minister to the Argentine Republic went through the Senate without opposition. He made the journey to Buenos Ayres via Paris, where he had his wound examined by the famous surgeon, Nelaton, because no American surgeon would undertake the removal of the bullet from under his cheek-bone. Dr. Nelaton could not tell him more than the American surgeons had told him, and the leaden memento from Marianna, which he carried in his head, became the cause of his untimely death two years later. He was then only a short distance from his native land, which, under the protection of the stars and stripes, he could have entered without molestation. He longed to visit his parents' grave, to see his only sister, to meet his old comrades; but that peculiar pride which many of the exiles felt, prevented him from setting foot on Hungary's soil before she was free again.

In Buenos Ayres he acquitted himself of his new duties so creditably that after seven months' service he was appointed also minister to Uruguay, and held both posts until his death, January 21, 1868. The President of the Argentine Republic ordered extraordinary military and civil honors to be paid at his funeral, and his remains were sent to the United States, where they rest in Arlington National Cemetery.

Part VI

In the Armies of the Ohio, Cumberland and Tennessee there was also quite a number of Hungarians who distinguished themselves. First among them was Brig. General Albin Schoepf, who commanded a brigade of three regiments in the division of Gen. Thomas in Eastern Kentucky, with which he successfully repulsed the attacks of about 8,000 Confederates under Gen. Zollicoffer near Mill Springs until Gen. Thomas could come to his aid, January 19, 1862. It was an important victory which caused great rejoicing in Washington, for it opened Cumberland Gap and Eastern Tennessee to the Federals. The Senate at once confirmed Gen. Schoepf's appointment, which had been before it for four months.

The career of Gen. Schoepf is an interesting illustration of the hardships and the opportunities of the American immigrant. He had received a thorough military education at an Austrian military academy, joined the Honvéd Army and, after the catastrophe, had to flee the country. He arrived in America penniless and friendless, a stranger in a strange country, and, unable to speak the language of the country, had to take a job as porter in a fashionable Washington hotel, carrying the baggage of the patrons. His noble cast of features and his gentlemanly bearing attracted the attention of Joseph Holt, then Patent Commissioner, who, on hearing his story, procured a small position for him in the Patent Office. Through his intelligence and faithful work he gradually advanced, and, when Holt became secretary of war in Buchanan's cabinet, was transferred to the War Department. There he could use his military education and experience to good advantage, and his abilities were recognized even by Lieut. Gen. Scott[xviii]. It was probably due to. the influence of Holt that, soon after the beginning of the war, he was appointed brigadier general and given a command in Holt's home state, Kentucky. In September, 1862, he was entrusted with the command of a division in the 3d Army Corps under Gen. Gilbert. The following year he became commander of Fort Delaware, on Pea Patch Island, near Newcastle, which was used as a Federal prison. After the war, he returned to the Patent Office, and was chief examiner there until his death in 1886.

George Pomucz, ex-honvéd captain and farmer in Iowa, enlisted in the 15th Iowa Infantry and, as major, commanded a brigade in the 17th Army Corps. He was wounded in the battle of Shiloh, and breveted brigadier-general for gallant and meritorious service.

Frederic Knefler, *recte* Knöpfler, rose from first lieutenant to colonel of the 79th Indiana Infantry and brevet brigadier-general. He was assistant adjutant-general to Gen. Lew Wallace at Shiloh, was conspicuous for bravery at Chickamauga, and was twice commander of a brigade. Gen. Knefler was an Hungarian Hebrew, born at Arad, and he was the only Hebrew to achieve the rank of brigadier general in the United States[xix].

We have already heard of Géza Mihalóczy, in a preceding chapter, as captain of the Lincoln Riflemen. Hardly had he left for Cairo, Ill., when his friend and fellow-exile, Julian Kuné, was requested by a deputation of German-Americans to organize a regiment, which he did. This regiment became the 24th Illinois Infantry, and the Lincoln Riflemen, having been recalled by special permission of Gen. McClellan, were incorporated into it. Mihalóczy was its lieut. colonel and, afterwards, its colonel, Kuné its first major; two other Hungarian officers in the regiment were Major Augustus Kováts and Captain Alexander Jekelfalussy.

Mr. Kuné, after a successful career in politics, journalism and business, was induced to publish a volume of reminiscences last year[xx]. It is interesting reading and throws many sidelights also on the lives of other exiles. He had been a honvéd lieutenant, followed Gen. Bem to Aleppo and came to America in 1852. Sympathetic friends helped him to lessen the hardships which every immigrant has to go through; he settled in Chicago, became affiliated with the Board of Trade, was active in politics and journalism, and was war-correspondent for the Chicago Tribune in the Franco-Prussian War.

He was ordered with the 24th Illinois Infantry to Alton, but soon returned to St. Louis to organize a company of mounted artillery. Owing to the intrigues of Col. Hecker, he was prevented from rejoining his regiment, and resigned toward the end of the year.

The 24th Illinois Infantry, under the leadership of Col. Mihalóczy, made a glorious record for itself, and fought in all the important engagements in Tennessee. At Chickamauga Mihalóczy was shot through the hand while waving his sword to encourage his men. About midnight on February 24, 1864, he went to the front at Buzzard

Roost Gap, Tenn., to make, as was his wont, a personal inspection of the picket line, when a single shot was fired, which wounded him dangerously in the right side. An investigation was ordered, but it could never be ascertained whence the shot had come. He died of his wound at Chattanooga March 11, 1864, and was buried there in the National Cemetery[xxi].

Nicholas Perczel de Bonyhád organized and commanded the 10th Iowa Infantry. He had had a very prominent part in the Hungarian revolution, both as a politician and a soldier, having been a member of the diet and commander of the fortress of Arad.

Andrew Gállfy was major of the 58th Ohio Infantry, and had the misfortune to be captured at the battle of Chickasaw Bayou, Miss. He was exchanged, however, and was later on detached service on the gunboat Mound City.

In the Department of the Gulf, where Gen. Asbóth commanded the District of West Florida, several Hungarian officers were engaged in organizing the Corps d'Afrique or United States Colored Troops. Among them was Peter Paul Dobozy,

who organized the 4th U. S. Colored Heavy Artillery, and became its lieut.-colonel. He was being educated for the priesthood, when the Hungarian revolution broke out ; he ran away from the seminary and enlisted as a honved. He was severely wounded when fighting in the Hungarian Legion in the Austro-Italian War, and was still suffering from his wounds when he arrived in the United States in 1861. ' He is now eighty years old, and is a respected citizen of West Plains, Mo.

Col. Ladislaus L. Zsulavszky, a nephew of Kossuth, organized the 82d U. S. Colored Infantry at Port Hudson, La., and commanded the first brigade in the District of West Florida. Two other Zsulavszkys, probably his brothers, served in the same regiment as lieutenants: Emil A. and Sigismund Z. The latter died of disease during the war. Joseph Csermelyi, a former honvéd lieutenant, was major of the same regiment, while A. P.

Zimándy served as lieutenant in the 4th U. S. Colored Cavalry.

In the 1st Florida Cavalry there appear to have been four Hungarian officers: Major Albert Ruttkay, probably one of Kossuth's American nephews, and Captains Alexander Gaal, Emeric Mészaros and Roland T. Rombauer.

Captain Alexander Gaal belonged to the de Gyula branch of the Gaals, which is famous in Hungarian history for the many great soldiers it has given the country. One of the family, Peter Gaal de Gyula, raised a regiment of Hungarian and Croatian carbineers for Wallenstein, which had an important part in the battle of Dessau [1626]. Another, Nicholas, was a general in the Honvéd Army in 1849, and was sentenced to twenty years in an Austrian dungeon, where he lost his eyesight and died in 1854. Alexander Gaal himself was a lieutenant in the Honvéd Army, and was severely wounded in one of the engagements. After the catastrophe he fled to Turkey, but was induced by a promise of immunity to return to Hungary. He was seized, however, and pressed into the Austrian Army as a private. In 1863 he joined the Polish revolutionists, but fell into the hands of the Russians who turned him over to Austria. At that time Austria was endeavoring to reconcile Hungary; so they let him go free on the condition that he leave the country. He then came to the United States, enlisted in the Federal army, and, after the war, made his home in Louisiana.

Figure 5 Col. Charles Zágoni

Part VII

In the eastern campaigns — in fact, in the whole Union Army — no native of Hungary achieved more than Julius H. Stahel, who, in less than two years, rose from lieut.-colonel to major-general and from the command of a regiment to that of an army corps, and received from Congress the medal of honor.

He was born in Szeged, in the heart of the Hungarian Lowland, on November 5, 1825. In America he was often believed to have been a Count Sebastiani, and McClellan thought his name had been Count Serbiani. How this legend originated is unknown, as his Hungarian name had been Számvald. As quite a young man he kept a bookshop in Pest, and it was he to whom Petöfi wrote his poem, Egy Könvárus Emlékkönyvébe [For the Souvenir-Book of a Bookseller]. He naturally espoused the patriotic cause, joined the Honvéd Army, served under Gen. Guyon as lieutenant, and was wounded at the battle of Branyiszkó. He was also awarded the Cross of Bravery by the Hungarian Government. After the revolution, he found refuge first in England, then in the United States, where he arrived in 1856 and engaged in journalism, working on the staffs of Lexo's Belletristische Zeitung and the New York Illustrated News,

In response to Lincoln's first call for volunteers, he, with Louis Blenker, at once began to organize the 8th New York Infantry, of which he was elected lieut.-colonel. His American baptism of fire he received in the first battle of Bull Run, July 21, 1861, where his regiment was part of the reserve at Centreville. At first the Union force had the best of it, but in the afternoon a reverse set in, which ended in their utter rout. Stahel was commanded to cover the retreat, and formed his regiment in line of battle on both sides of the road. In this position he was twice attacked by the enemy's cavalry, which he repulsed each time, and held his position until the following morning, when he received orders to fall back on Washington. He reached the Potomac in the evening, bringing with him all the field pieces the flying troops had left on the road, also two stands of Union colors.

Figure 6 Julius H. Stahel, Major General, USV

It is evident that but for the firm stand and resistance of Stahel's command the enemy could have followed up the retreating Union Army to Washington, for the official report of the Confederate commander, Gen. Johnston, says: "The apparent firmness of the United States troops at Centreville checked our pursuit"[xxii]. When the report of the conduct of Stahel's regiment reached headquarters, both President Lincoln and Lieut.-General Scott sent for Blenker and Stahel, and expressed their appreciation and gratitude for the protection of the rear of the army at a time when all apprehended a furious assault from a pursuing enemy.

In recognition, Stahel was commissioned colonel and was entrusted with the organization of a regiment of heavy artillery. He was appointed brigadier-general in

November, 1861, and was placed in command of a brigade in the Army of the Potomac under Gen. McClellan. Next April his brigade was transferred to the Army of West Virginia to the command of Gen. Rosecrans, and in May to that of Gen. Fremont at Petersburg, a change which both he and Gen. McClellan sincerely regretted. On June 1 Stahel's advance came upon Gen. Jackson's rear guard near Strassburg, where he engaged the enemy, driving and following him up, until ordered by Fremont to halt. A week later the battle of Cross Keys was fought with great obstinacy and violence until dusk, where both armies rested on their arms, Stahel's command having borne the brunt of the fight.

In the second battle of Bull Run, August 29 and 30, 1862, in which he commanded Schenck's division, it fell to his lot again to cover the retreat of the Union Army. Towards the end of November he encountered the enemy at Ashley Gap and at Snickers Gap, and after a sharp fight drove him across the Shenandoah River, pursuing him so rapidly that he surprised a cavalry regiment in camp and captured many prisoners, horses and the regimental colors.

In January, 1863, he was given the command of the 11th Army Corps, but soon yielded it to Carl Schurz. In March he was promoted to major general and, by the express wish of the President, was assigned to the command of a cavalry division in front of Washington. Toward the end of the year he was transferred to the Department of the Susquehanna, where, for the protection of Harrisburg, the capital of Pennsylvania, he concentrated and organized the cavalry, which was distributed all over the state.

The following spring he was again transferred to the Department of West Virginia in command of the 1st Cavalry Division, and led the advance column down the Shenandoah Valley. He drove the enemy across the river near Mount Jackson, and took part in the battle of New Market. On June 5, near Staunton, he was ordered by Gen. Hunter to charge the Confederate cavalry and check its advance. On the first charge Gen. Stahel broke the enemy and pursued him as far as Piedmont, where he found the main force of the Confederates in a strong entrenched position, and held them there until the arrival of Gen. Hunter with his army. Hunter soon commenced the attack, and ordered Stahel, whose troops were somewhat exhausted, to form the reserve. The battle raged furiously for some time, when Stahel received orders to dismount three of his cavalry regiments and send them to the support of the infantry. He lead this dismounted force himself into action, was badly wounded, and taken to the rear to have his wound dressed. While he was in the surgeons' hands, Gen. Hunter expressed great regret and disappointment, for he wanted Stahel to charge the enemy's flank, while he would attack the front in full force. Gen. Stahel, seeing the need of a quick, concerted and strong action, told Hunter that he would lead the charge. So he had his wound dressed to stop the bleeding and, being helped to mount his horse as he had no use of his left arm, he charged with his entire mounted force the enemy's flank, dislodged him from his entrenched position and created a general stampede. For his heroism at Piedmont he was awarded by Congress a medal of honor, the highest distinction an American soldier can receive. Being invalided for several months, he was ordered to Baltimore, where he did duty as president of a General Court Martial, until he resigned from the army in February, 1865.

In his military career he had risen rapidly, and gained the confidence and respect of his superiors, which they never had cause to regret. He was now to show his fitness for an entirely different and, to him, new line of work in the public service. There had been many irregularities in the consulate at Yokohama, Japan, and Secretary of State Seward selected him, in 1866, for the task of reorganizing that consulate, bringing it to a satisfactory status, and entering into arrangements with the Japanese authorities for the opening of new ports. Stahel was eminently successful in both directions; he reorganized the consulate on a basis of efficiency, and in 1869 the ports of Osaka and Hiogo were thrown open to American commerce.

He then returned to the States and became interested in some mining concerns in the West. In 1877 he was sent again to Japan as U. S. Consul at Osaka and Hiogo, which post he held until appointed consul-general at Shanghai, China, in 1884. He was twice temporarily detached and entrusted with special duties of a delicate nature in the Far East. He also sent the State Department lengthy reports and recommendations as to the reorganization of the service in the Far East, with particular reference to the judicial system; they formed the basis of several reforms which were subsequently carried out. Incessant work and an uncongenial climate having impaired his health, Stahel resigned in 1885, and returned to New York where he became connected with one of the largest financial institutions of the country.

Unlike his friend, Alexander Asboth, he was blessed with a long life, and thus had more opportunities to bring his abilities into full play. He lived up to his high ideals of honor and duty, he was a cheerful companion and a loyal friend, and, in a delicate and unostentatious manner, did much to help his less fortunate brethren. He visited Hungary during the Millennium in 1896; and among his souvenirs of an eventful life there was none which he valued more highly than a picture of Louis Kossuth with his autograph dedication. He died in New York on December 4, 1912, and was buried in Arlington National Cemetery with full military honors.

Part VIII

The Garibaldi Guard, or 39th New York Infantry Regiment, was the most cosmopolitan organization in the War for the Union. It was composed of Hungarians, Germans, Italians, Frenchmen, Spaniards and men of various other nationalities, but the Hungarians had a plurality over any of them and constituted nearly one-half of the regiment. This gave it something of an Hungarian character, which came to expression also at the presentation of colors.

Figure 7 Presentation of Hungarian colors to the Garibaldi Guard, New York, May 23, 1861

Three flags were presented: An American, an Hungarian, and an historical Garibaldi flag.

On one side of the Hungarian, red, white and green standard was the motto, within a wreath, Vincere aut morire; and on the opposite side, in English, the same motto. Conquer or die. The regimental name appeared on each side, over and underneath the wreath, in English. This elegant present was from Miss Grinnell. It had four beautiful silk pendants of colors and inscriptions, the latter embroidered as follows: White, Sylvia Grinnell; red, Presented to the Garibaldi Guard; blue, New York, 23d May, 1861; red, white and blue, Brethren before, brethren again[xxiii].

At the beginning of the war many regiments chose showy or fanciful uniforms, the general favorite being the costume of the Zouaves. Reading the papers of that period, one gets the impression that each state must have furnished at least half a dozen Zouave regiments. The uniform of the Garibaldi Guard was something unique, being modeled after that of the Italian Bersaglieri, and they wore hats with big cock-feathers. They were a soldierly-looking lot, and carried their flags with honor all through the eastern campaigns, their list of battles including: First Bull Run, Cross Keys, Gettysburg, North Anna, Bristow Station, Po River, Mine Run, Spottsylvania, Wilderness, Tolopotomoy, Coal Harbor, Petersburg, Strawbury Plains, Ream's Station, and Deep Bottom.

The first colonel of the regiment was an Hungarian, Frederic George Utassy; among the other Hungarian officers were Major Anthony Vékey, Captains Victor Sándory, Francis Takács and Anthony Utassy, and Lieutenants Louis Tenner, Charles Utassy and Charles Zerdahelyi.

Zerdahelyi came from a noble family, and was a pupil of Liszt and a pianist of some note. He was a captain in the Honvéd Army, and was entrusted by the Hungarian Government with a confidential mission to Germany; but on his way thither he was captured by the Austrian police, and kept in a dungeon at Kufstein in heavy irons for two years. Through his refined manners and accomplishments as a musician he made many friends among cultured Americans, and supported himself as a teacher of music[xxiv]. But the horrors of Kufstein had left an indelible mark of sadness on his genial face.

Quite different in temperament was his close friend, Col. Philip Figyelmessy, a true representative of the Hungarian hussar at his best. He was handsome, chivalrous, dashing, reckless, of winning manners; and his devotion to Kossuth was little short of adoration. He had been a major of the Bocskay Hussars, and, having belonged to the garrison of Komárom, received a safe-conduct, with which he could stay in Hungary. But he soon aroused the suspicions of the Austrian police, and had to flee the country. Kossuth trusted him implicitly, and sent him on several important missions to Hungary. He entered the country in various disguises, as a Galician Jew or a Servian pig dealer, and, although he had some hair- breadth escapes, he always managed to deceive the Austrian police. One day in 1853 he was taking breakfast with Capt. Mayne Reid in London, when the latter, glancing at a paper, noticed a news item according to which "the famous emissary, Figyelmessy" had been captured in Hatvan and hanged. It turned out later that it was a Capt. Thury, with a fatal likeness to him, who had been mistaken for him by the watchful Austrian police and actually hanged.

Through his connection with Kossuth and Pulszky he became acquainted with many prominent Britons, and his exploits and adventures were so much talked about in London at that time that Edwin Lawrence Godkin — who had written a history of Hungary[xxv] and was then connected with Cassel's publishing house — offered to write a story of his life with the Hungarian struggle for independence as the background.

In Italy, in 1859, Figyelmessy was Kossuth's aide-de-camp. The following year he organized and commanded a squadron of Hungarian hussars, with which he fought through Garibaldi's Sicilian campaign. He treasured to his last day a letter from Garibaldi, in which the latter wrote of him as the bravest of the brave.

Finding the prospects of a renewal of the war and of carrying it into Hungary gone, he came to America in 1861 to offer his sword to the Union. He was well supplied with letters of introduction, among which was one from Kossuth to Secretary Seward. He did not think much of the volunteers, and declined the colonelcy of a regiment of dragoons on that account. All his compatriots belonged to the volunteer force; but he was commissioned colonel in the regular army, and was ordered to report to Gen. Fremont at Wheeling, who made him inspector-general. Later he became inspector-of-outposts to his countryman and friend, Gen. Stahel.

He did also a few Hungarian hussar stunts during the war, as when he "with only fifteen men brilliantly charged and put to flight a body of cavalry commanded by Ashby in person[xxvi]. But he suffered a double hernia in an accident, which troubled him a great deal and hampered him in his movements for some time.

After the war, he was rewarded with a consulship, and he chose Demerara, in British Guiana, which post he kept under various administrations from 1865 to 1888. One of his consular reports on the evils of coolie labor attracted wide attention in Great Britain, and the agitation which followed it, did much toward the amelioration of the condition of the coolies. In his last years he lived in Philadelphia, and longed to see his native land once more; but, true to his word, he would not set foot on her soil unless she was independent.

He died in 1907 at the age of eighty-five[xxvii].

Figure 8 Philip Figyelmessy, Colonel, USA

Among his friends was Emeric Szabad, who had been a government official during the Hungarian War, fled to England, served in Figyelmessy's Hungarian squadron in Sicily, and came to America early in 1862[xxviii]. Here he got a commission as captain, and was made inspector of outposts to Gen. Sickles, whom he had known in London. He had the ill-luck to be captured and put into that place of horrors, Libby Prison. His happy disposition made him a favorite, and even won the good-will of Turner, the jailer, who allowed him to write to Figyelmessy. In this letter the prisoner described himself as in danger, through sheer hunger, of eating his dilapidated boots.

Figyelmessy and Gen. Stahel responded with a box of eatables, which arrived safely at its destination and was delivered intact. After his release from Libby, Szabad returned to the front, and was breveted colonel for gallantry in the battles before Petersburg. The war ended, he went to Texas as assistant collector of the port of Galveston.

Col. Cornelius Fornet had gone through many vicissitudes before the Civil War. He was an engineer, served in the Honvéd Army with the rank of major, and was decorated for gallantry. With great difficulties he made his way to America, and first assisted Prágay in writing his book. In 1850 he went with three fellow-exiles, Count Samuel Wass, Gustave Molitor and John Juhos, to California, where they met with some success in the gold fields. Being skilled engineers they found it, however, more profitable to coin the gold that others had dug up, and, having obtained a government license, operated a mint for that purpose under the firm of Wass, Molitor and Company. In 1852 Fornet went to Bruxelles to wed his fiancee, from whom he had been separated through the war, and returned with her to New Jersey, where they founded their home. In the Civil War he was first a major of engineers in Fremont's Army of the West. Having received serious injuries in an accident at Camp Lily, near Jefferson City, he was sent East, and after his recovery was ordered by Gen. Halleck to organize the 21st New Jersey Infantry Regiment, of which he became the colonel.

In the eastern campaigns were also engaged Brig.-Generals Kozlay and Mundee, Col. Korponay, Majors Décsy, Stephen Kovács and Semsey. Captains Menyhárt and Rózsafi, and several others, whose names and records can be found in the appendix.

There were several officers in the Union Army, who, while not natives of Hungary, may be classified as Hungarians, for they had been identified with the Hungarian cause, spoke the Hungarian language, and attached themselves in America to the Hungarians. Among them were: Constantin Blandovski, a Pole, who had served in the Honvéd Army, and was captain in the 3d Missouri

Infantry. He was mortally wounded at the capture of Camp Jackson, near St. Louis, May 10, 1861, and died fifteen days later. — Nicholas Dunka, a native of Jassy, Rumania, who had been Figyelmessy's lieutenant in Sicily, and accompanied him to America. He was an aide on Gen. Stahel's staff with the rank of captain, and a brave soldier, though always in trouble on account of his uncontrollable temper. He lost his life in the battle of Cross Keys, Va., June 8, 1862, and was buried there in the yard of the Union Church. — George von Amsberg, a native of Hannover. He entered the Austrian service as an officer of a crack Hungarian hussar regiment, and got there so Hungarianized that he spoke Hungarian in preference to German, went over with his regiment to the Honvéd Army, and fought for Hungarian independence. In the Civil War he was colonel of the 45th New York Infantry.

Part IX

The services of Hungary's sons for the preservation of the Union seem not to have been limited to the military field. It is impossible at the present time to determine the full importance of what Louis Kossuth has done to prevent the threatening intervention of Great Britain, because the documents relating thereto are still inaccessible ; but it is evident that Kossuth did use his influence in behalf of the United States at that critical period.

When Louis Kossuth came to America in 1851, one of his warmest admirers and supporters was William H. Seward, then senator from New York. What his friend and partner, Horace Greeley, did for Kossuth and the Hungarian cause in the Tribune, Seward tried to do on the floor of the Senate and in the realm of politics.

At the outbreak of the Civil War, Great Britain's attitude towards the United States was anything but friendly. Lord Palmerston — who, in 1849 had refused to acknowledge victorious Hungary, a thousand-year-old nation, as a belligerent — had no such scruples in regard to the Confederate States, which had won no victories as yet and were but the embryo of a nation never to be born; he was, in fact, in very great haste to acknowledge them. During the excitement of the Trent affair. Great Britain openly made warlike preparations, and, although an armed conflict was then averted, grave apprehensions were entertained in Washington lest Great Britain, and, perhaps, France also, would intervene.

It is known that Secretary of State Seward "conceived the idea of sending to Europe, in an unofficial capacity, three representative and influential men to meet the impending danger of foreign intervention. He chose for this mission Archbishop Hughes, Bishop McIlvaine and Mr. Thurlow Weed"[xxix]. It is less well known that he also sought to enlist the aid of Louis Kossuth.

This was a very natural idea, for, while he could not know then the inner history of Kossuth's relations to Napoleon and Cavour, he did know that, in 1859, Kossuth had prevented the intervention of Great Britain in the Austro-Italian conflict through his speeches at public meetings in England and Scotland and his influence with the British Liberals, which caused the downfall of Lord Derby's cabinet[xxx].

Seward had a great liking for the gallant and straightforward Col. Figyelmessy, who had brought him letters from Kossuth and Pulszky, and of whom he knew that he had the confidence of Kossuth. One day in February, 1862, he asked Figyelmessy, if he would be willing to go to Genoa, and requested Kossuth to use his influence with the Liberals of England and suggest to them the expediency of beginning an agitation in favor of non-intervention, by holding public meetings and through the press. Figyelmessy consented, and went a few days later again to the State Department for his final instructions. Seward was then very much encouraged by the latest news from the West, and thought the voyage would be unnecessary for the present. Later he came back to his original design, when Figyelmessy suggested that it would be just as well to state the facts by letter, as this way he would not lose the spring campaign and Kossuth would surely not require any persuasion to act. The suggestion being approved, Figyelmessy wrote the letter, and Kossuth returned an answer which the Secretary of State said was "very satisfactory.[xxxi]

In the Austro-Italian War it was quite proper for Kossuth to make public speeches in Great Britain against intervention, for that war was in close connection with the aspirations for Hungarian independence, of which he was the acknowledged representative; but no such connection existed with the American Civil War. His agitation, therefore, was restricted to one by private correspondence only.

In the five volumes of Kossuth's letters, which have been published, there is no reference to the subject. A large part of his correspondence, however, is still unpublished, and is deposited in the Hungarian National Museum, in Budapest. In reply to my inquiries I was informed that it will not be accessible to investigators until fifty years after Kossuth's death, i.e. 1944. Thus there is little chance of obtaining more information on the question until that time, unless some letters should turn up from, other sources.

A PARTIAL LIST OF HUNGARIAN OFFICERS IN THE UNION ARMY DURING THE CIVIL WAR

GENERAL OFFICERS

ASBOTH (Asbóth), Alexander

Bom in Keszthely Dec. 18, 1811. In the Honvéd Army col. of engineers and aide to Gov. Kossuth. With Kossuth

in Kutahia.

Col. 2nd Mo. Inf., May, 1861; Gen. Fremont's chief -of-staff and appointed by him brig.-gen. Sept. 3, 1861, which was not recognized and ceased as such March, 1862; brig.-gen. March 31, 1862; commander of District of Columbus, 1862; of District of West Florida, 1863. Wounded at Pea Ridge March 7, 1862, and at Marianna Sept. 27, 1864.

Breveted major-gen. for gallant and faithful service during war March 13, 1865. Mustered out August 24, 1865.

U. S. Minister to Argentine Republic 1866 and also to Uruguay, 1867. Died in consequence of wounds in Buenos Ayres Jan. 21, 1868. Buried in Arlington National Cemetery.

KNEFLER {Knöpfler) , Frederic

1st It. 11th Ind. Inf. April 24, 1861; capt. June 5, 1861; capt. asst. adj.-gen. Oct. 21, 1861; major May 16, 1862; col. 79th Ind. Inf. Sept. 28, 1862; breveted brig.-gen. March 13, 1866, for gallant and meritorious service during war; mustered out June 7, 1865.

Died in Indianapolis June 15, 1901.

KOZLAY, Eugene

Bom 1828. Capt. in Honvéd Army. Enrolled Aug. 30, 1861, at Hudson City, N. J.; col. 54th N. Y. Inf. Oct. 16, 1861 ; brevet brig.-gen. March 13, 1865, for gallant and meritorious service during war; mustered out April 14, 1866. Died April 1, 1883.

MUNDEE (Mándy?), Charles

Enrolled in Kansas. Capt. asst. adj.-gen. Aug. 24, 1861; major Aug. 16, 1862; breveted col. Oct. 19, 1864, for gallant conduct in the battles of Winchester, Fisher's Hill and Cedar Creek; breveted brig.-gen. April 2, 1865, for gallant and meritorious service before Petersburg; mustered out Sept. 15, 1866. Died June 4, 1871.

POMUTZ (Pomucz), George

Born 1826. Capt, in Honvéd Army. 1st lt. 15th Iowa Inf. Dec. 23, 1861; wounded at battle of Shiloh April 7, 1862; major June 3, 1863; lt.-col. March 23, 1865; breveted brig.-gen. March 13, 1865, for gallant and meritorious service during war; mustered out July 24, 1865. Died Oct. 12, 1882.

SCHOEPF, Albin

Honvéd officer. Brig.-gen. Sept. 30, 1861; commander of Fort Delaware 1863; mustered out Jan. 15, 1866. Chief examiner in U. S. Patent Office. Died May 10, 1886.

STAHEL (Számvald), Julius H,

Bom in Szeged, Nov. 5, 1825. 1st lieut. in Honved Army; wounded in battle of Branyiszko. Received Cross of Bravery.

Lt.-col. 8th N. Y. Inf. May 13, 1861; eol. Aug. 10, 1861; brig.-gen. Nov. 12, 1861; commander of 11th Army Corps Jan 15, 1863; major-gen. March 14, 1863; ref^gned Feb. 8, 1865. Awarded medal of honor Nov. 4, 1893, for having led his division after he was severely wounded at Piedmont, June 5, 1864.

U. S. consul at Yokohama 1866-1869; U. S. consul at Osaka and Hiogo 1877-1884; U. S. consul-general at

Shanghai 1884-1885. Died in New York Dec. 4, 1912; buried in Arlington National Cemetery.

STAFF AND LINE OFFICERS

ALBERT, Anselm

Lt.-col. in the Honved Army; with Gen. Bem in Aleppo.

Lt.-col. 3d Mo. Inf. April 22, 1861; col., aide-de-camp July 12, 1861; col., Gen. Fremont's chief -of-staff March 31, 1862.

CHANDORY (Sdndory), Victor

Capt. 39th N. Y. Inf. May 28, 1861; resigned Sept. 10, 1861.

CORMANY (Kórmány), George N.

Private 6th Ohio Inf. June 8, 1861; sergeant March 1, 1862; 2d It. Feb. 14, 1863; 1st It. April 1, 1864; mustered out June 23, 1864.

CSERMELYI, Joseph

Lieut, in Honved Army.

Capt. 45th N. Y. Inf. Aug. 25, 1861; resigned Oct. 2, 1862; capt. and brevet major 82d U. S. Colored Inf. Jan. 9, 1863; mustered out Sept 10, 1866.

DETSHY (Decsy), Edward

Lieut, in Honved Army.

Major add. aide-de-camp June 16, 1862; mustered out Dec. 14, 1866.

DOBOZY, Peter Paul

Bom in Szombathely 1832; lieut. in Honved Army; officer of the Hungarian Legion in Italy.

Lt.-col. 4th U. S. Colored Heavy Artillery June 16, 1863;

DOLEZICH, Charles

Sergeant 9th Ohio Inf. May 27, 1861; 1st It. July 24, 1862; on detached service Dec. 9, 1862; mustered out June 7, 1864.

ESTI, William M.

Bom 1826.

2d It. 26th Ohio Inf. Dec. 17, 1861; 1st It. Dec. 5, 1862; resigned April 5, 1863.

FIALA, John T.

Bom in Temesvar 1822; major in the Honvéd Army; with Gen. Bern in Aleppo.

Lt.-col. 2d Mo. Inf., U. S. Reserve Corps, May 7, 1861; col., chief top. eng. Sept. 20 to Nov. 19, 1861; col, add. aide-de-camp March 31, 1862; resigned June 8, 1864. Died in San Francisco Dec. 8, 1911.

FIGYELMESSY, Philip

Bom in Pest Jan. 1, 1822; major of Bocskay Hussars in the Honved Army ; aide-de-camp to Louis Kossuth in Italy; lieut.-col. of Hungarian Legion in Italy.

Col. U. S. A., inspector-general to Gen. Fremont March 31, 1862; inspector of outposts to Gen. Stahel March 25, 1863; resigned Dec. 20, 1864.

U. S. Consul at Demerara, British Guiana, 1865-1888; died in Philadelphia July 25, 1907; buried at MaHetta, Pennsylvania.

FORNET, Cornelius

Major in Honved Army.

Major of eng. in Mo.; wounded at Camp Lily, near Jefferson City, in Oct., 1861; col. 21st N. J. Inf. Sept 1, 1862; resigned Dec, 1862.

GAAL (Gadl) , Alexander

Lieut, in Honvéd Army. Pressed into Austrian Army as private. Took part in Polish Revolution of 1863. Captured by Russians.

Capt. 1st Fla. Cavalry (no date) ; resigned Nov. 27, 1864. Died in New Orleans, La., February 29, 1912; buried in Chalmette National Cemetery.

GALLFY, Andrew {Gállfy Gállik Endre)

Bom 1821; officer in the Honved Army.

Enrolled Oct. 2, 1861; capt. 58th Ohio Inf. Jan. 8, 1862; major Oct. 20, 1864; captured at battle of Chickasaw Bayou, Miss., Dec. 29, 1862; detached on U. S. gunboat Mound City from May 22, 1863, to Aug. 1, 1863; mustered out Jan. 4, 1865.

HASKELL, Leonidas

Capt., aide-de-camp to Gen. Fremont Sept. 20 to Nov. 19, 1861; major, add. aide-de-camp June 16, 1862; resigned June 4, 1864. Died Jan. 15, 1873.

JE KELFALUSY, also JE KALFALURY (Jekelfalussy), Alexander

Enrolled June 29, 1861; 1st lt. 24th 111. Inf. July 8, 1861; capt. July 3, 1862 ; mustered out Aug. 6, 1864.

KORPONAY, Gabriel de

Honvéd officer.

Lt.-col. 28th Penna. Inf. June 28, 1861; col. April 25, 1862; discharged on surgeon's certificate March 26, 1863.

KOVACS (Kovács), Stephen

Bom in 1823. Major in Honvéd Army; with Kossuth in Kutahia.

Enrolled Sept. 7, 1861, as capt. of Barney Rifles at Hudson City. N. J.; capt. 54th N. Y. Inf. Sept. 23. 1861 ; major June 3, 1862; captured and paroled prior to March 11, 1864 ; mustered out April 14, 1866.

KOVATS (Kováts), Augustus

Honvéd officer.

Lt. Lincoln Riflemen Feb., 1861; capt. 24th Ill. Inf. July

8, 1861; severely wounded at Jasper, Tenn., June 12, 1862; resigned on account of wounds Jan. 19, 1863; breveted major.

KUNÉ Julian

Born in Belényes in 1831. Lieut, in Honvéd Army; awarded medal of third class; with Gen. Bem in Aleppo.

Enrolled June 17, 1861; major 24th 111. Inf. July 8, 1861; resigned Oct. 31, 1861.

MANYHARDT, Joseph

Capt. 45th N. Y. Inf. Aug. 25, 1861; resigned June 14, 1862.

Seems to be identical with Menyhdrt G. János, honvéd lt. (mentioned in Lászlo's Napló-Töredékek, page 138, and in Pesti Hirlap, Jan. 4, 1907), who died in Brooklyn, N. Y., in Dec, 1906.

MAYTHENY (Majthényi), Theodore

1st sergeant 2nd Iowa Inf. May 28, 1861; transferred to Fremont's Body Guard Aug. 21, 1861 ; 2d lt. Sept. 15, 1861 ; mustered out Nov. 30, 1861; capt. 1st Ind. Cav. April 18, 1862; mustered out Dec. 13, 1864; 2d It. 6th Cav., U. S. A., Feb. 23, 1866; 1st It. Oct. 20, 1866; resigned Dec. 23, 1868.

MESZAROS (Meszdros), Emeric

Honvéd officer.

Major 4th Mo. Cav. (Fremont Hussars) May 18, 1861; capt. 1st Fla. Cav. June 27, 1864.

MIHALOTZY (Mihaldczy), Geza

Honvéd officer.

Capt. Lincoln Riflemen Feb., 1861; It. col. 24th 111. Inf. July 8, 1861; col. Dec. 23, 1861; shot through hand at Chickamauga Creek, Tenn., Sept. 19, 1863 ; shot at Buzzard Roost Gap, Tenn., Feb. 24, 1864; died of wound at Chattanooga, Tenn., March 11, 1864; buried there in National Cemetery.

MOLITOR, Albert

1st lt. 13th Battery, N. Y. Light Artillery Oct. 15, 1861; resigned Dee. 8, 1862.

NEMETT (Németh), Joseph

Capt. in Honvéd Army; with Kossuth in Kutahia.

1st lt. 5th Mo. Inf. May 18, 1861; mustered out Aug., 1861; col. 5th Mo. Cav. (Benton Hussars) Feb. 14, 1862; honorably discharged by reason of consolidation with 4th Mo. Cav. Nov. 15, 1862.

PERCZEL, Nicholas

Born in Bonyhád 1812. M. P., col. in Honvéd Army; commander of Fortress of Arad; with Kossuth in Kutahia.

Col. 10th Iowa Inf. Sept. 1, 1861; resigned Nov. 11, 1862

PETRI, Charles

Major 16th Ill. Inf. Aug. 6, 1862; declined commission as lt.-col.; mustered out Jan. 21, 1865.

POKORNY, Anthony

Major 8th N. Y. Inf. April 23, 1861; It.-col. 7th N. Y. Inf. Nov. 12, 1864.

REMINYFY (Reményfy?), Joseph

Capt., aide-decamp on Gen. Fremont's staff, July 12, 1861.

May be misprint for Kemenyfi, for there was a honvéd officer by that name among the refugees.

ROMBAUER, Raphael Guido

Sergeant 1st Mo. Inf., U. S. Res. Corps May 7, 1861; major 1st Ill. Light Art. March 25, 1864; mustered out Oct. 26, 1864. Died at Kirksville, Mo., 1912.

ROMBAUER, Robert J.

Born 1830. 1st lt. of Art. in Honvéd Army; pressed into Austrian Army as private.

Lt.-col. 1st Mo. Inf., U. S. Res. Corps, May 7, 1861 ; col. Sept. 12, 1861.

ROMBAUER, Roderick E.

Bom 1833. Capt. 1st Mo. Inf., U. S. Res. Corps, May 7, 1861; aide-de-camp on Gen. Fremont's staff in 1862.

ROMBAUER, Roland T.

Born in Munkács, 1837. Sergeant 1st Mo. Inf. April 22, 1861; provost marshal of District of West Florida; capt. 1st Fla. Cav. Aug. 27, 1864; mustered out Nov., 1866.

ROSAFY, Ernest M. (Rózsafi Mátyás)

Born in Komarom, 1828. Honved officer.

Capt. Battery B, W. Va. Art., Oct. 1, 1861; honorably discharged April 18, 1862. Clerk in U. S. Bureau of Census. Died in New York, 1893.

RUTTKAY, Albert

Capt. 3d U. S. Colored Heavy Art. June 16, 1863; major 1st Fla. Cav. Aug. 24, 1864; honorably discharged May 31, 1865.

SEMIG {Simig?) , Bernard Gustave

Private 9th N. Y. Inf. May 4, 1861 ; hospital steward U. S. Army, May 20, 1863; medical cadet July 2, 1864; asst. surgeon Nov. 10, 1874. Died Aug. 11, 1883. .

SEMSEY, also SEMPSEY (Semsey), Charles

Born in Karácsonmezö 1830. 1st lt. of Art. in Honvéd Army; capt. in British Army in Crimean War.

Capt. 20th N. Y. Inf. May 6, 1861; resigned June 6, 1861; major 45th N. Y. Inf. Aug. 25, 1861; resigned June 14, 1862. In U. S. Customs Service; chairman of Board of Special Inquiry in U. S. Immigration Service at Ellis Island. Died in New York 1911.

SERINI (Szerényi), Philip

2d lt. 8th N. Y. Inf. April 23, 1861; transferred to 2d Battery N. Y. Art. Sept. 1, 1861; resigned June 4, 1862.

Seems to be identical with Szerényi Antal, honvéd captain, who was with Kossuth in Kutahia.

SZABAD, Enteric

Secretary in War Department in Hungary. In Hungarian Legion in Italy.

Capt., aide-de-camp to Gen. Sickles June 16, 1862; captured and in Libby Prison ; breveted lt.-col. March 13, 1865 ; breveted col. March 26, 1865, for gallant conduct in the battles before Petersburg ; mustered out Oct. 7, 1865. Assistant Collector of the port of Galveston.

TAKATS (Takács), Francis

Born 1826. Captain in Honvéd Army.

Capt. 39th N. Y. Inf. May 28, 1861; discharged Nov. 19, 1861.

TAUSZKY, Rudolf

Assistant surgeon Sept. 24, 1863; mustered out July 27, 1865. Captain in Honvéd Army. Died September 21, 1889.

TENNER, Louis

2d lt. 39th N. Y. Inf. May 28, 1861; capt. 7th N. Y. Inf. Aug. 27, 1861; resigned April 15,1862.

UTASSY, Anthony Von

Born 1831. Honved officer.

1st lt. 39th N. Y. Inf. Sept. 1, 1861; capt. Sept. 22, 1862. Died in Philadelphia Feb. 15, 1911.

UTASSY, Carl Von

2d It. 39th N. Y. Inf. June 1, 1862; 1st It. Sept. 22, 1862; mustered out May 31, 1863.

UTASSY, Fred. George De

Born 1827. Honvéd officer. Enrolled May 17, 1861; col. 39th N. Y. Inf. May 28, 1861; dismissed May 29, 1863.

VANDOR (Vándor), Joseph

Captain in Honvéd Army.

Col. 7th Wisc. Inf. June 24, 1861; resigned Jan. 30, 1862.

WAAGNER (Wagner), Gustave

Major of Art. in Honvéd Army; with Kossuth in Kutahia.

Col., instructor of art. at Cairo, 111., May, 1861 ; chief of ordnance on Gen. Fremont's staff July 12, 1861 ; col. 2d N.Y. Art.

WEEKEY, also VEKEY (Vékey), Anthony

Born 1833.

1st lt. 39th N. Y. Inf. May 28, 1861; capt. July 15, 1861; major Feb. 1, 1862; died April 28, 1862, in hospital at Winchester, Va.

ZAGONYI, also SEAGOYNE (Zágonyi), Charles

Born in Szatmár 1826. Capt. of Hussars in Honvéd Army.

Major Fremont's Body Guard, Mo. Cav., July 12 to Nov. 30, 1861; col, add. aide-de-camp March 31, 1862; resigned June 4, 1864.

ZERDAHELYI, Charles

Capt. in Honvéd Army; in Kufstein Prison. 2d lt. 39th N. Y. Inf. July 30, 1862. Died in Philadelphia, 1906. Buried in Holy Sepulchre Cemetery, Mount Airy, Philadelphia.

ZIMANDY (Zimándy), A. P.

2d lt. 4th U. S. Colored Cavalry Sept. 6, 1864.

ZULAVSKY {Zsulavszky), Emil A. Z.

1st lt. 82d U. S. Colored Inf. May 7, 1864; mustered out Sept. 10, 1866.

ZULAVSKY (Zsulavszky), Ladislas L.

Col. 82d U, S. Colored Inf. Nov. 1, 1863; commander of 1st Brigade, District of West Florida; mustered out Sept. 10, 1866.

ZULAVSKY (Zsulavszky) , Sigismund Z.

2d lt, 82d U. S. Colored Inf. Sept. 1, 1863; died of disease at Port Hudson, La., Sept. 16, 1863.

NOTES

---

[i] Most of the latter translators and commentators of the Heimskringla take Tyrker to have been German. The question hinges on the translation of the Icelandic words "á thyrsku." It is difficult to see how they can be translated with "in German" instead of "in Turkish." (Turk and Turkish were then the appellations given to the Hungarians and their language.)
[ii] Senate Document No. 279, 61st Congress, 2nd Session. See also Senate Document No. 48. 81st Congress. 1st Session.

[iii] *The Hungarian Revolution,* by Johann Prágray. New York, G. P. Putnam. 1850. 12-mo., 177 pp. An abridged German edition was simultaneously published by J. Helmich, New York, under the title *Der Krieg in Ungarn.*

[iv] A full account of this expedition by Louis Schlesinger, one of the participants, can be found in the Democratic Review for Sept., Oct., Nov. and Dec, 1852. The final installment of the series, dealing with the fate of some of the prisoners in Ceuta. was not published, because the magazine was discontinued. In Hungarian the matter is ably treated by Dr. Géza Kącziány in the Szabadság, Cleveland, Dec. 21. 1911. The Hungarians in the party were: John Prágay, as lieut.-general and chief-of-staff; Major Louis Schlesinger, Captain Radnics, Lieutenants Bontila, Eichler and Palánk, and Privates Biró, Nyikos and Virág.

[v] *War Pictures from the South.* New York, Appleton's. 1863. 8-VO., VIII, 352 pp. This is a cheap reprint of the London edition in two volumes. The German edition was dedicated to Gen. McClellan, a rather strange proceeding on the part of a Confederate officer.

[vi] "We meet everywhere here, in town and country, Italians, Hungarians, Poles, Magyars, Jews and Germans, who have come to us from that empire, but no one has ever seen a confessed Austrian among us." Seward to

Anson Burlingame (Minister to Vienna), April 13, 1861, in *The Diplomatic History of the War for the Union*. Boston. 1884. Page 214.

[vii] Investigations in the Military and Anthropological Statistics of American Soldiers. By Benj. Apthorp Could, New York. 1869. Page 87.

[viii] Stated to me by Gen. Julius Stahel.

[ix] *Reminiscences of an Octogenarian Hungarian Exile*. By Julian Kuné. Chicago, 1911. Page 98.

[x] *McClellan's Own Story*. By George B. McClellan. New York

[xi] *The Contest*. By R. J. Rombauer, St. Louis, February 1, 1863. 16-mo., 100 pp

[xii] *The Union Cause in St. Louis in 1861*. By Robert J. Rombauer, St. Louis, 1909. 8-vo., XIV, 475 pp. The appendix contains the rosters of the St. Louis regiments.

[xiii] The History of a Life by Roderick E. Rombauer, St. Louis, 1903. 8-vo., 146 pp.

[xiv] "A shameful number of regular officers had deserted; those who remained were nearly all on duty east of the Mississippi Valley; and the difficulty of officering and rendering efficient the masses of untrained troops was a serious embarrassment. Fortunately our adopted citizens recognized that Freedom was of no nationality; and the swords that had been used in its behalf in Germany and Hungary were taken down and offered to aid in saving its very hearth-stone, as the United States had seemed to them." Mrs. Fremont in *The Story of the Guard*, Page 28.

[xv] The best account of the battle was written by Major W. Dorsheimer, of Fremont's staff, in The Atlantic Monthly for Jan., Feb. and March, 1862, under the title "Fremont's. Hundred Days in Missouri" It contains a plan of the field and many incidents and sidelights on Asbóth and Zágonyi. It was largely drawn upon by the earlier historians of the Civil War, as Greeley, Abbott, etc.

[xvi] The Story of the Guard. By Jessie Benton Fremont, Boston, 1863. l2-mo.. XII-229 pp. It contains Zigonyi's own report, too.

[xvii] The Pea Ridge Campaign. By Franz Sigel. in *Battles and Leaders of the Civil War. I*, 328.

[xviii] *Frank Leslie's Illustrierte Zeitung*, February 8, 1862.

[xix] *The American Jew as Patriot, Soldier and Citizen.* By Simon Wolf, Philadelphia, 1895. Page 179.

[xx] *Reminiscences of an Octogenarian Hungarian Exile* by Julian Kuné, Chicago, 1911. 12-mo., VIII-216 pp.

[xxi] *Report of the Adjutant-General of the State of Illinois.* Springfield. Ill, 1886. Volume II.

[xxii] *Rebellion Record.* Series I, II. 478.

[xxiii] Harper's Weekly, June 8, 1861.

[xxiv] There are many interesting reminiscences about Zerdahelyi and other Hungarian exiles in The Life and Public Services of George Luther Stearns, by Frank Preston Stearns, Lippincott's, Philadelphia, 1907. It appears that there was a little Hungarian Club in Stearns' home-town, Medford, Mass., and Mr. Stearns and his friends extended much sympathy and help to the Hungarian refugees. Besides Zerdahelyi. Col. and Mme. Thuolt, Capt. (Stephen) Kinizsi, "General Kalapkur," the Rev. "Achs," and M. and Mme. Zulavsky are mentioned by name, I do not know the evolution of the name Thuolt. "General Kalapkur" — for whom George Luther Stearns, Henry W. Longfellow and others organized a riding school, and who seems to have been an impostor — was perhaps identical with John Kalapka, Lieutenant of Hussars, who had been, with Kossuth at Kutahia. The Rev. "Achs," whose Unitarian leanings seem to have pleased Mr. Stearns a great deal, was none other than Gideon Acs, Kossuth's chaplain. Being a fine oriental scholar, he gave a course of lectures on Egypt and the Assyrians.

---

xxv The History of Hungary and the Magyars, By Edwin Lawrence Godkin, New York, 1853. 8-vo., 380 pp. A reprint of the English edition.

xxvi Rebellion Record. Series I. V. 2l. June, 1881.

xxvii Figyelmessy's memoirs were written by his wife, née Eliza Haldeman, during his lifetime, but not published. I had the privilege of reading the manuscript, and had also the pleasure of a personal acquaintance with the colonel.

xxviii Szabad was a man of literarv and scholarly attainments. He wrote: Hungary Past and Present', Edinburgh, 1854; Hungarian Sketches in Peace and War (a translation of some of Jokai's stories), Edinburgh, 1854; The State Policy of Modern Europe, 2 vols., London, 1857; and Modern War. New York, 1863.

xxix The Diplomatic History of the War for the Union. By William H. Seward, Boston, 1884. Pages 6 and 7.

xxx The matter is fully treated in Kossuth's *Memories of My Exile*, New York, 1880. pp. 188-276.

xxxi From Figyelmessy's unpublished memoirs. The Colonel had also related the incident to me personally.

FIN

CPSIA information can be obtained
at www.ICGtesting.com
Printed in the USA
BVHW031946020520
579088BV00002B/412